Identity

Aisha Khatun

BookLeaf Publishing

Presentation by *BookLeaf Publishing*

Web: www.bookleafpub.com

E-mail: info@bookleafpub.com

ISBN: 9789357212809

First edition 2023

*For my dear Abba. Not a moment passes when I
do not think of you.*

ACKNOWLEDGEMENT

Thank you to my sister, for which without her, this short collection of poems would not be possible. You are my rock in this chaotic world we call life.

The Uncle post dinner walk

The uncle post dinner walk,
Where politics is left inside,
At the table,

Existing only for dinner talk
The heated discussions over pilau, samosas and
chai
Leave our bodies, as the earth takes a deep
breath,
And mother nature sighs

The difference in opinions,
From left to right
Come to an end
Where day meets the silence of night

Have Sabr

'Have sabr. Have sabr.'
'Be patient. Be patient.'
The standard response to our pain

Patience is a virtue. At what cost?
When did being patient,
become synonymous with being meek?

When did having sabr,
become synonymous with repression?

At what cost did our mothers,
Our grandmothers,
Our great grandmothers,
pay for having sabr in the way
we have been told to have sabr
for generations upon
generations

To be patient is a beautiful quality,
To persevere in the face of agony,
With grace, with smile
And humility
Is what makes us, us

But to be in pain,
To exist insufferably,
To see and know only darkness
To be in conflict with oneself
And then to hear 'Have sabr'
is no means to an end

A London summer

A London summer,
brings long days and short nights,
Joy, laughter, evening bike rides
Cold beers and iced teas,
Thames river walks with a cool breeze

Laying in the grass upon golden hour
Cool nights with quenching showers
Ice creams from park vans
Lips meeting the coolness of a can

The 9-5's seem slightly less boring
The commute not so soul consuming
The warmth awaits the day's workers
Turning each dishevelled shell into believers

A London winter

A London winter,
brings short days and long nights

Solitude, silence and ease of mind
Hot chocolate, mulled wine,
Christmas markets and frost bite

Winter wonderland and flashing lights
Autumn's cousin, yesternight

Every night

Every night
When we close our eyes
Our body cools as we say goodbye

The roaring of engines quieten down
The day birds no longer make a sound

For though it is quiet,
The darkness though silent
Is very much alive

The rustles of trees
The footsteps on leaves
Little etches on the ground
Owls no longer home bound

Every night we enter the land of dreams
Our minds wandering in deep sleep
Our souls are set free
Our bodies still, in ease

The hustle and bustle of the day
Far gone, left astray
For this brief moment, whilst we lay
Our cells restore and rejuvenate

When darkness falls,
we leave this physical world
To enter a different plane
Sinking with each deep breath
And with the light of morn,
Only to rise again

In the land of dreams

In the land of dreams
Skies are orange and blue,
Birds of paradise fly askew

Deep sunsets fill the atmosphere
Etches of honey, amber and crimson
Guide the wandering traveller

Passing river streams,
Hearing the gush of water falls
To find to whom we belong

As day turns into night
And darkness fills the land
We find our person,
Our people,
The warmth and comfort,
Of a familiar hand

Our loved ones,
The dearly departed.
A friend, a parent,
A grandparent,
Existing in harmony
Smiling with joy,
In peace, in ease

For there is no pain
In the land of dreams,
Amongst the ancestral plane

Where skies are golden,
And nights are indigo blue.
Shooting stars fill the yonder,
Where the wondering traveller
is free to ponder

Rejoicing in memories past of joy and glee
Free to come and go,
Whenever and wherever
they please

Ulcinj

Ulcinj, the little town
That never sleeps

With fresh seafood,
and endless ice cream

Apple spritz and sun
Nude female beaches
Iced lattes and messy hair buns

Bridget Jones and tiramisu
Metaphorical caves,
Endless beaches,
Waters so blue

Golden skin and freckled cheeks
Laziness, brain mush
Tanning on the beach

Cool breezes and bright lights,
Dancing with the locals,
Chaotic days,
Serene nights

Falamendearing our week away
Taking deep breaths,
Passing castle walkways

Endless hills and sloping steeps
Laughter and joy with
the best company to keep

This is a goodbye

This is a goodbye,
to the person who once was

The decay and rot of the past
No longer hold us in its grasp

This is a goodbye,
to the person who couldn't say no

To malicious people, adamant
on stunting your growth

This is a goodbye,
to the person who was broken

The weight of the world,
Swallowing them whole,
Made them become unspoken

This is a goodbye,
to those who were fallen
Burnt and from the ashes, they rose
Never to be unforgotten

This is a goodbye,
to our previous selves,
Our passive bodies, dying
with our skin cells

This is a goodbye,
to whom you no longer are

Be yourself, be true
You have come so far
Embrace the new

Ghosts of the past

The fire within
As a child it begins
Isolated, alone
All behaviours,
Frowned upon

Pushed aside,
Made hidden away
Fading into the background
With each and every day

The solitude of play
provides no peace
When your mind
is never at ease

The ones whom we seek
Our role models and carers
Turned abusers and scarers

Reality is harsh, cruel and cold
To the books we go,
Recreating ourselves,
Allowing us to mould

As time goes by,
We leave the past behind
Recreating ourselves
But within our subconscious mind

The ghosts of the past
leave their finger prints
their hold on us,
forever imprinted in parts

The lonely boy

Loved by some
Heard by none
Sad and alone
The forgotten son

The black sheep
The object of critique
The disrespected and unheard
The clipped winged bird

So sombre and restrained
A hardened heart
With wild spirit tamed

Life is a rollercoaster

Hold onto the ones who light your soul
Who see the darkness within and stay
Who accept you whole
As well as fragmented and debased

For those who only dwell in joy and laughter
When the warmth disappears
And the gloom takes after
Are the first to turn and sneer

What use is it to be in a full room
Indulging in celebratory cheers
When those same chums turn glum
At the verge of melancholic tears

Having one person accept you for you
Through the highs and lows
Is more enriching than a hundred untrue
For life is a rollercoaster, not a plateau

Who you once were

Who were you?
Before the world told you who to become?
Does that little voice speak to you,
encompassed within a soul so glum?

Buried within,
Hidden upon layers of masks and facades
Taught that to merely exist as you are
Your very nature is humanely flawed

Your inner child
calls to your aid
Tamed from being unruly and wild
Misery and disdain
plagues them

Hear their voice
As they tell you
Go back to the days of blue skies
Yellow suns with huge rays
existing in semi circles
on the corner of a page

Go back to running through grass
rolling down hills

dirtying your face.
Weeds in your hair
Before the world taught you
your place

Before your voice and your spirit
was taken from you.
Placed in a little box
locked up with a key
Never to be heard
Nor seen

Cover your hair

Cover your hair, that's what good girls do
Wear modest attire,
Men will not misconstrue

To be covered is to be protected
Averted from the eyes of men
Rejected by some, though eternally respected

Cover your hair and lower your gaze
Avert your eyes
Lower your face

You are free from their wants
You do not exist
Worldly desires do not taunt

For you are a good girl
Who prays and supplicates
A rare and beautiful pearl
Who speaks to no men,
And certainly does not date

The only man who enters your home
Is your brother and Qur'an teacher
A once in a while family figure
A respected community preacher

Cover your hair, that's what good girls do
Recite louder from the diaphragm
Like I have showed you

Here is 'a helping hand'
Fingers and body shakes
For this is no ordinary man.

The loss of innocence and youth
In the supposed safety of a home
A young girl in one year of mourning
Of her dearly departed father's soul

Cover your hair, don't be home late
Stay true to yourself, do not deviate
Boys are untrustworthy
To be around them is to be dirty

All the showering in the world
could not wipe off the dirt
Burning skin under hot water
Turning this boisterous girl
Into a shadow.

Don't cover your hair

Cover your hair, don't cover your hair
Wear a bra, don't wear a bra
Wear the niqab, jilbab and abaya
Wear whatever you please.
We teach women their freedom.
'You are a pearl to not be touched'
Ultimately,
To be yourself is liberation.
Having autonomy
of one's body
is to be woman and free.
Our mannerisms and attire,
so heavily policed
regardless of what we wear.
Contrary to popular belief,
sexual assault and harassment
is not about desire.
It is about control.
Any and every space
within a matter of seconds
can become unsafe.
Take precaution,
but know,
arguing over laced thongs in courts
and short skirts
is a stupid dand pointless exhaustion.

To love is to feel

We all undergo a journey

Where we lose ourself.
Some experience it late,
some experience it early

Amidst long summer days
or cold winter nights,
As seasons change
along it we sway

A loss of who we once were.
So naive and so intoxicated.
Falling for our very saboteurs.
Malleable hearts, eyes fixated.

Who knew love could be so cruel?
We're told,
with pain comes growth.
Turning us all into ironic fools

The apple of our eyes
soon turns sour.
It's sweet disguise
does devour

Our humanity clings.
For love is not enough,
when our ears bleed
and hearts ring

To love is to feel.
To love oneself,
that is to heal

Infatuation draws us near.
Acceptance of reality
makes everything clear,

Like a beautiful tree,
love grows of its own accord,
deep from the roots
to the tips of luscious leaves

Etched into our very beings,
it has many different forms
and perceived meanings

For it can only grow
in the right conditions

Giving us a healthy glow
Or a slow deterioration

Broken trust

Trust takes years to build
And only seconds to break

To walk away is to be strong-willed
Closed eyes become fully awake

Years of reliability and being true
Shattered within seconds

Subverting our point of view
Reminding us to check in
with oneself

Acknowledge the painful reality
Close some doors
Allow life to simply be
Do not be the fool and ignore

Broken trust is a terrible pain
We never fully recover
Questioning each bond,
Forever disdained

Like a broken mirror
Once shattered into pieces

The parts you recover
Will never look the same
As before

The knight in rusty, I mean, shining armour

We're told to want the knight
On horseback, in rusty, I mean, shining armour
To make everything alright
Swoon us, be quite the charmer

The handsome prince
So strong and so brave
Rescuing the damsel in distress
Trapped in a metaphorical cave

Free her from the villain's clutches
Break her from her chains
Heal her with your touches
Allow her to ride your mane

Okay we are going to stop right here
Because what the fuck is this
This dusty boy is not your saviour
These novels have me in bits

The closed door in front of you
Can be opened from the inside
Trust me. All you need is a screw
Or, just shove it aside
That will do

Go downstairs
Find the dragon's lair
Lure her in with your voice
Be gentle, no loud noise

You're a natural,
See how she beckons you
The creature of the supernatural
Jump on her back and come through

Off you set,
Take it all in,
Admire the views

The knight in rusty armour
is still on his way
By the time he reaches the tower
Night will turn to day

The cushioned blow

The eldest daughter takes the full frontal blow
Always walking on eggs shells,
Heels never flat, constantly on mere tip toes

Never ending expectations
Unattainable standards
The community's neglected foundation

Nations are birthed from her very flesh
Birth rights, human rights and independence
wars
The very spine of the desh

She scrapes her skin
Bleeds herself dry
Takes the evil within
And hides her cries

She stomachs it all
Until she can no more
Breaking the cycle
And the rigid walls

She stands up to her oppressors
The hypocrites, the backbiters
The misogynists and aggressors

Slays them all one by one
Dismantling their notions
Destroying their hold
Shattering the mould

She walks so that you can run
The forgotten soul
But the kindest, loving
And boldest of all